Knowing the Notes

for bass

by Cassia Harvey
edited by Matthew Roberts

CHP135

©2005 by C. Harvey Publications All Rights Reserved.

www.charveypublications.com - print books
www.learnstrings.com - PDF downloadable books
www.harveystringarrangements.com - chamber music

Knowing the Notes for Bass
The Note D; open string

Cassia Harvey

Yankee Doodle

Traditional/arr. C. Harvey

How many D notes are in this song?

The Note E

The New World and Variation

How many E notes are in this song?

Dvorak/arr. C. Harvey

How many beats are in a measure?

The Note F#

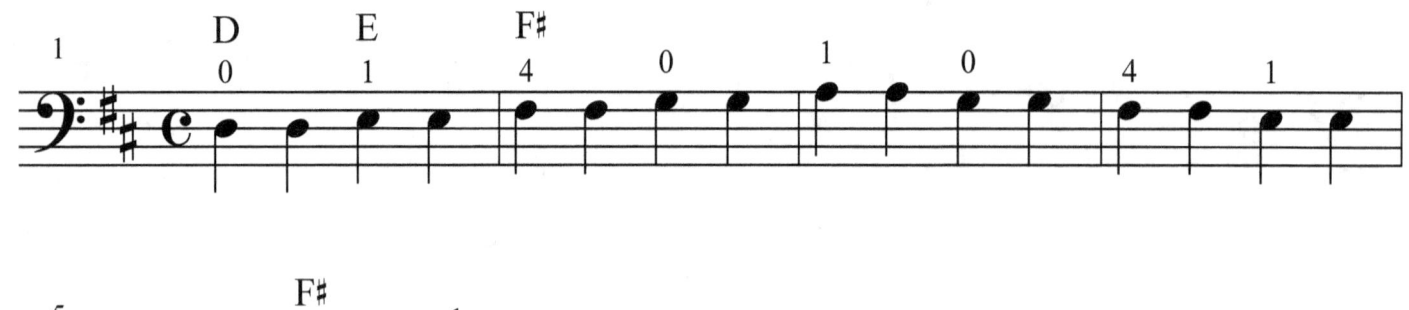

Dance with Variation

How many F# notes are in this song?

Praetorious/arr. C. Harvey

The Note G; open string

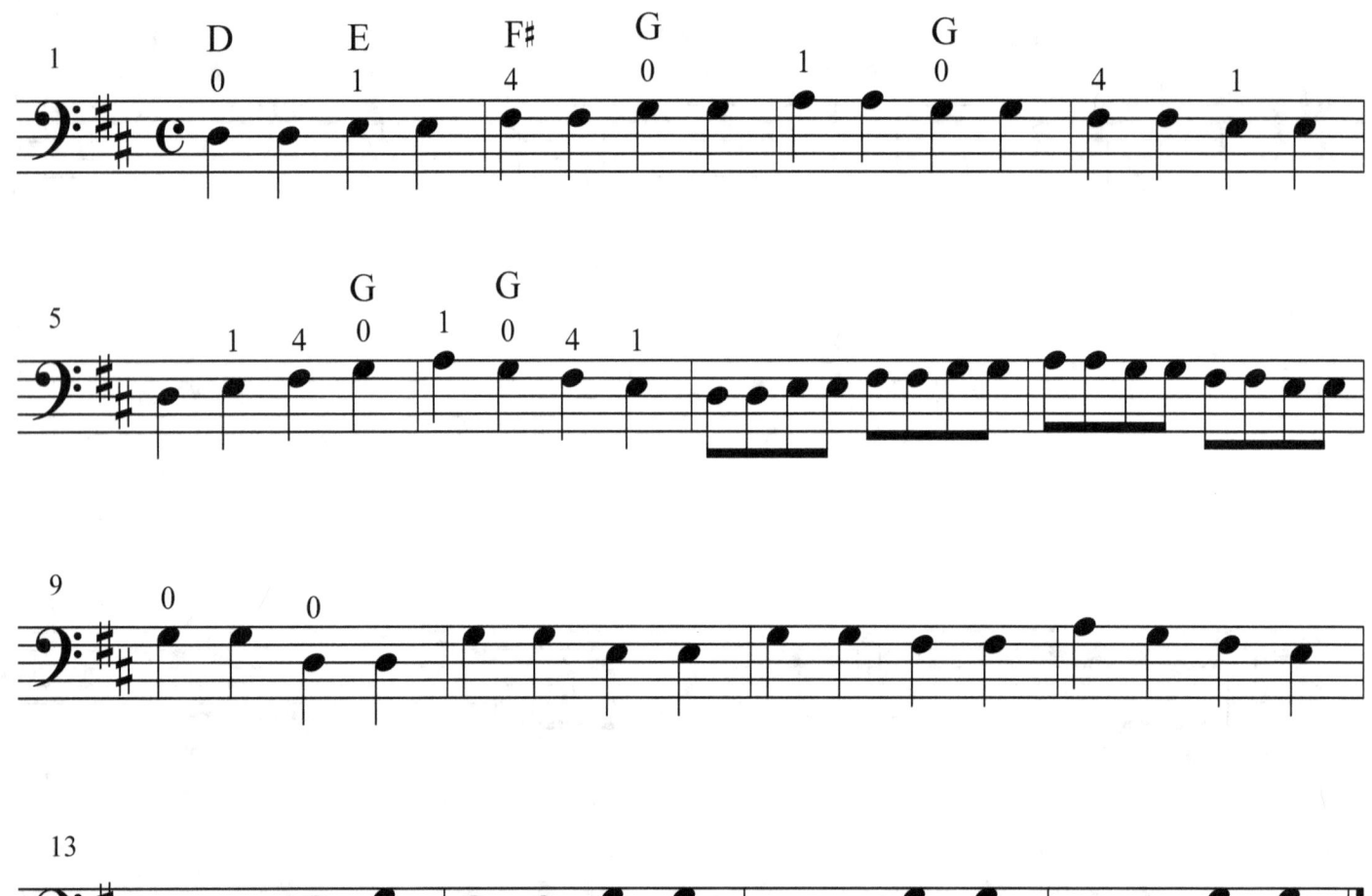

French Dance

How many G notes are in this song?

Traditional/arr. C. Harvey

The Note A

Allegretto

Campagnoli/arr. C. Harvey

How many A notes are in this song?

How many beats are in a measure?

The Note B

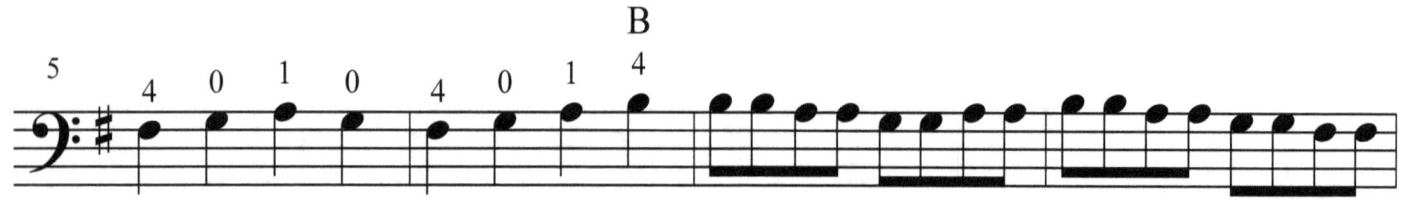

Lavender's Blue

Traditiona/arr. C. Harvey

The Note F♮

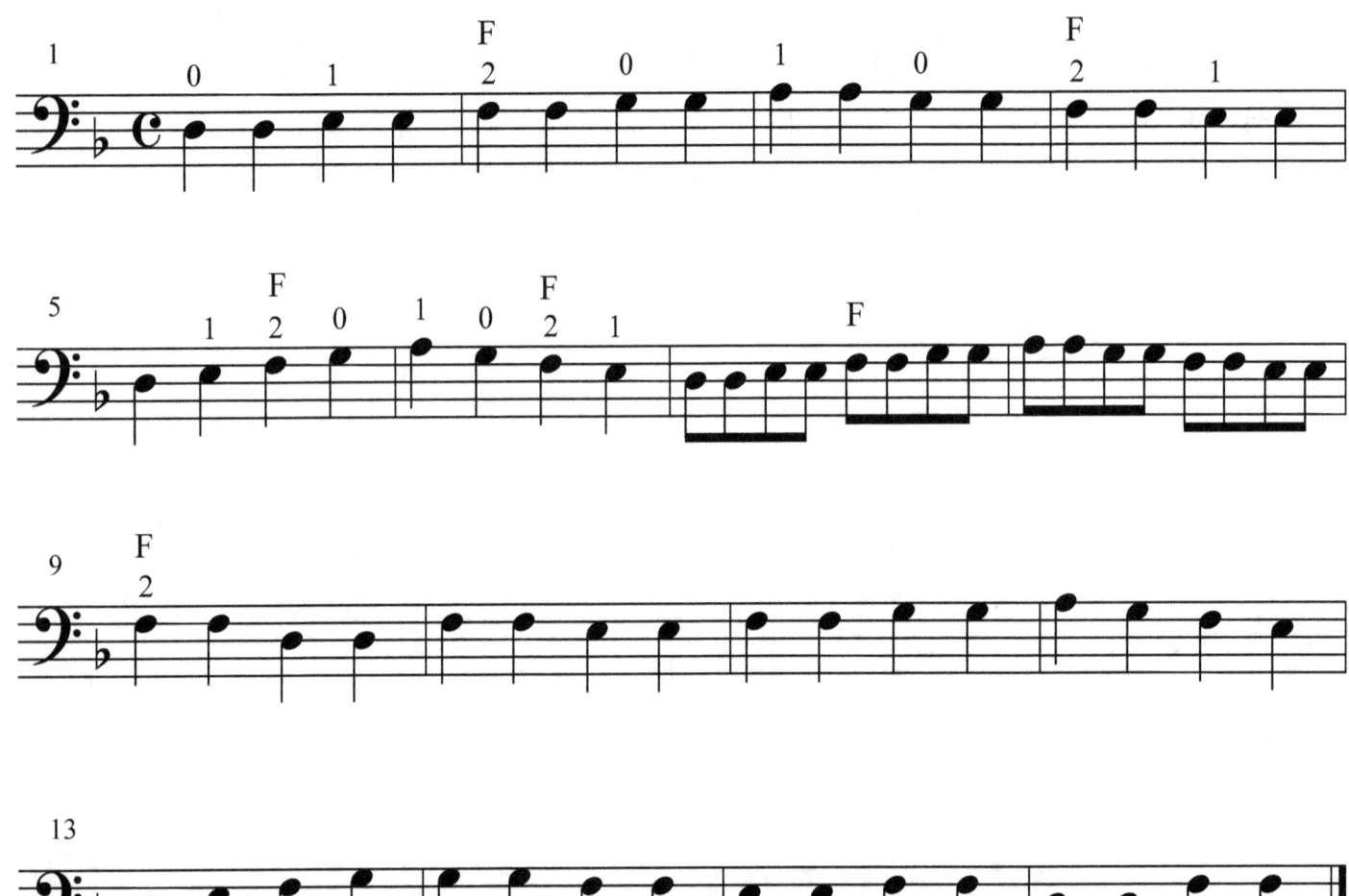

Farandole

Bizet/arr. C. Harvey

The Note B♭

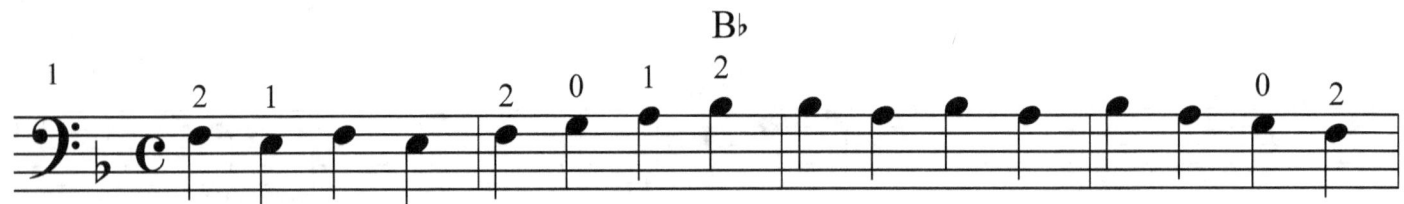

Aiken Drum

Traditional/arr. C. Harvey

The Note A; open string

Soldier, Will You Marry Me?

Traditional/arr. C. Harvey

The Note B

Drill, Ye Tarriers, Drill

Traditional/arr. C. Harvey

The Note C#

Cassia Harvey

©2005 C. Harvey Publications All Rights Reserved.

The Prince of Denmark's March

Clarke/arr. C. Harvey

The Note C

Cassia Harvey

Little Dance

Turk/arr. C. Harvey

©2005 C. Harvey Publications All Rights Reserved.

Knowing the Notes for Bass

The Note E; open string

Cassia Harvey

The China Figurine

Rebikov/arr. C. Harvey

©2005 C. Harvey Publications All Rights Reserved.

Knowing the Notes for Bass

Goober Peas
Traditional/arr. C. Harvey

Old Joe Clark
Traditional/arr. C. Harvey

©2005 C. Harvey Publications All Rights Reserved.

Michael Rowed the Boat Ashore

Traditional/arr. C. Harvey

What Do You Do With a Drunken Sailor

Traditional/arr. C. Harvey

Knowing the Notes for Bass

Clementine

Traditional/arr. C. Harvey

The Caissons Go Rolling Along

Traditional/arr. C. Harvey

©2005 C. Harvey Publications All Rights Reserved.

www.ingramcontent.com/pod-product-compliance
Lightning Source LLC
Chambersburg PA
CBHW051430070526
44584CB00023B/3670